Action Art

Painting

Isabel Thomas

www.raintreepublishers.co.uk
Visit our website to find out more information about **Raintree** books.

To order:
 Phone 44 (0) 1865 888112
Send a fax to 44 (0) 1865 314091
Visit the Raintree Bookshop at **www.raintreepublishers.co.uk** to browse our catalogue and order online.

First published in Great Britain by Raintree,
Halley Court, Jordan Hill, Oxford OX2 8EJ,
part of Harcourt Education.
Raintree is a registered trademark of Harcourt
Education Ltd.

Editorial: Melanie Copland, Kate Buckingham
and Lucy Beevor
Design: Jo Malivoire and AMR
Picture Research: Mica Brancic
Production: Duncan Gilbert
Originated by Modern Age
Printed and bound in China by South China
Printing Company

ISBN 1 844 21239 4 (hardback)
09 08 07 06 05
10 9 8 7 6 5 4 3 2 1

British Library Cataloguing in Publication Data
Thomas, Isabel
Painting – (Action Art)
750
A full catalogue record for this book is available
from the British Library.

Acknowledgements
Corbis pp. **5**, **19** (Ariel Skelley); Cumulus pp.
10, **13**; GettyImages pp. **8**, **14**, **18** (Taxi);
Harcourt Education pp. **6**, **9**, (Trevor Clifford);
pp. **4**, **7**, **11**, **12**, **15**, **16**, **17**, **20**, **21**, **22**, **23**, **24**
(Tudor Photography)

Cover photograph of paint pots reproduced with
permission of Getty (Photographers Choice)

Some words are shown in bold, **like this**. You can find them in the glossary on page 23.

Contents

What is art?

Art is something you make when you are being **creative**.

People like to look at art.

A person who makes art is called an artist.

You can be an artist too!

What kinds of art can we make?

We can draw and paint pictures.

We can make collage and prints, too.

Sculptures are another kind of art.

Art can be big or small.

What is painting?

Painting is making a picture with paints.

Artists paint on special paper or card.

You can also paint something
that you have made.

These girls are painting a sculpture.

What kinds of paints can I use?

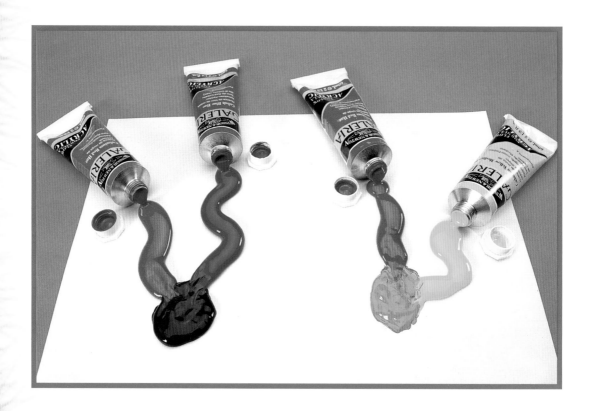

Some paints are ready to use.

You squeeze them out of a tube.

water

brush

powder paint

Some paints have to be mixed
with water.

You can make the paint thick
or watery.

What can I paint with?

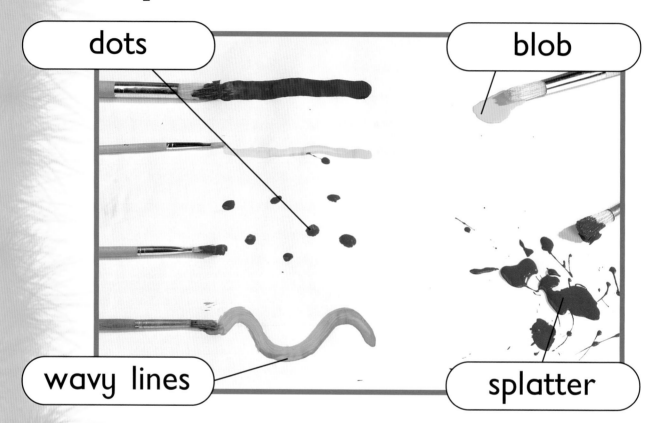

dots

blob

wavy lines

splatter

Most artists use **brushes** to make paintings.

Look at all the marks you can make with a brush!

apron

You can paint with your fingers, too!

Paints are messy, so wear old clothes or an **apron**.

13

What can I paint?

You can paint pictures of things that you see.

Choose places or **objects** that look interesting.

Look carefully at the colours and shapes.

Try to copy them.

What else can I paint?

Paint a picture of something that you like.

Plan what will be in your painting.

Think about a fun day, like a birthday.

Try to paint what you are thinking about.

How does painting make me feel?

Painting is fun. You feel happy when you are being **creative**.

When you show your paintings
to your friends, you feel proud.

Let's paint!

Let's paint a butterfly!

1. Fold a piece of paper in half and open it up again.

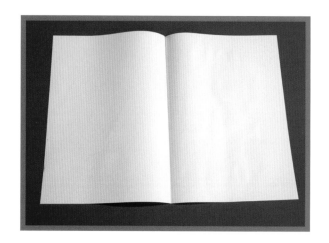

2. Paint a butterfly's wing on one side of the fold. Use lots of colours and patterns.

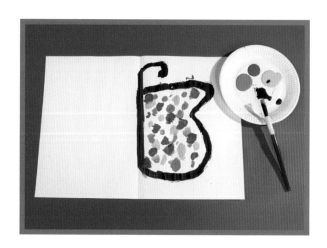

3. Fold the paper in half again while the paint is still wet. Press down hard.

4. Open up the paper again to find a **symmetrical** butterfly!

Quiz

All of these things are used for painting.

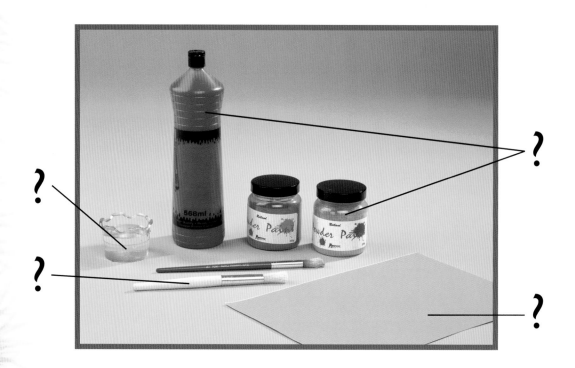

Can you remember what they are called?

Look for the answers on page 24.

Glossary

 **apron** piece of material that you wear to keep your clothes clean

 **brush** tool for putting paint on to paper. A brush has a handle and hairy bristles.

 **creative** making something using your own ideas and how you feel inside

 **objects** things that you can see and touch

 **symmetrical** when something looks the same on both sides

Index

Answers to quiz on page 2?

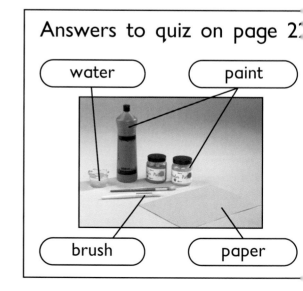

water

paint

brush

paper